This
My Magic Muffin
book belongs to:

_____

♡

This book is dedicated to my two beautiful daughter's,
Torrie and Carrie, who are the anchors in my life.

❤

First edition published Sept. 2017

All production designs are used under license.

My Magic Muffin®

Front cover and interior layout by C.G.Adler

ISBN

Book Two

Grandma Smiley's Magical Playmates

The 'My Magic Muffin' Family

Introducing:
Blueberry Muffin

By: C.G.Adler

What does the word magical mean? Magical is another word for remarkable, exceptional, amazing, stunning, incredible, unbelievable. All those words describe our magical muffins.

The stars in this story represent sparkle and magic.
The hearts represent love.

Grandma Smiley and Cinnamon Muffin are waiting for Anna, Peter, Samantha, and Ryan at the front door of her large house with the pretty pink and purple trim.

Today is sunny and bright with purple butterflies and red and yellow tulips fluttering in the breeze.

Grandma Smiley is sweeping her sidewalk while waiting for the grandchildren.

Cinnamon Muffin is sleeping quietly under the shade of the large green tree.

♡

When the children arrive for their weekly visit, they hurry to hug Grandma shouting, "Grandma, Grandma, It's a beautiful day."

Cinnamon Muffin is excited to see the children.

Cinnamon runs around in circles.
They all chase the puppy around and around the yard calling, "Cinnamon, Cinnamon, wait for us."

Cinnamon Muffin stops and looks at the children with a teasing glint in her eye.

She rolls in the soft, green grass. The children roll in the soft, green grass. They all run around in circles while shouting and laughing.

When the children and Cinnamon Muffin are tired of playing, they go into Grandma Smiley's kitchen and gather around the large, white wooden table with warm cups of cocoa topped with white mini-marshmallows and chocolate chip cookies.

"Yum, Yum, these cookies are so good Grandma," says Anna.

Grandma says "Thank you, Anna. Now, did you think about who your next playmate will be?"

"Yes, yes," the children answer together.

♡

"Banana Muffin would be a good friend," says Anna.

"Chocolate Muffin would be great," says Ryan.

"I like Strawberry Muffin," Says Peter.

Samantha quietly raises her hand and says "I think Blueberry Muffin would be just the right friend for Cinnamon to have."

The children vote on which playmate to make for Cinnamon Muffin.

Grandma Smiley calls out the names. She says, "Banana, Strawberry, Blueberry or Chocolate Muffin?"

The children raise their hands to vote, and Blueberry Muffin wins.

They all go to the kitchen. Grandma Smiley gathers the main ingredients for the muffin. Then she sets a large yellow bowl and a wooden spoon on the counter.

Anna and Samantha get the plump blueberries from the refrigerator. The blueberries wink their eyes at them and jump up and down while the girls try to catch them. Anna and Samantha's eyes grow large watching the blueberries.

"What is that?" says Samantha. Anna backs up as one blueberry springs up to kiss her on the nose. "WOW!" says Anna.

Peter and Ryan gather the shiny stars and red hearts. Peter puts magic stars in the yellow mixing bowl. Ryan adds red hearts of love.

All the children add one teaspoon of their love to the batter, and Grandma Smiley adds a pinch of her special magic.

The children take turns mixing the special batter with the large wooden spoon.

When Ryan is mixing, he says, "Grandma, my hands are getting tired." Just then, the batter begins to spin around and around in the shape of a tornado.

"YIKES," says Ryan as he grabs the bowl. The bowl dances on the counter and the spoon spins around in the mix. Clink! Clink! Clink! beats the spoon against the bowl. Ryan holds tight to the bowl.

Multi-colored stars explode in the air above the bowl. "Help me Grandma," says Ryan, "This is too heavy for me to hold."

ZIP!   ZAP!   ZINGO!

The magic begins to appear.

Grandma Smiley hurries to help Ryan hold the large, yellow bowl. The bowl is shaking, stars shoot into the air and out pops Blueberry Muffin. Ryan is so surprised his blue eyes nearly pop out of his head.

As Ryan holds tight to the large yellow bowl, a beautiful light blue puppy with dark blue sparkling hair on his tail, back, and ears begin to form above the spinning tornado. The puppy has large blue eyes, long black eyelashes, a soft red tongue, and a red heart nose.

The children become very excited while laughing and clapping their hands.

♡

Grandma Smiley sets Blueberry Muffin on the white table. The light blue puppy is smiling at the children, and her red heart nose is twitching a warm hello. Blueberry Muffin reaches out a paw to Grandma Smiley.

Oh, how happy the children are. They jump up and down calling "My Magic Blueberry Muffin."

Samantha. Anna, Peter, and Ryan hug and kiss the puppy. They dance around the table holding hands while laughing and singing "Blueberry Muffin, Blueberry Muffin, our new best friend."

♡

Cinnamon Muffin is in the Living Room where she is taking a nap. Grandma Smiley places Blueberry Muffin on the carpet next to Cinnamon Muffin. The two puppies look at each other and wag their tails. Their eyes sparkle. Their noses twitch. They jump around while yipping softly, as only puppies can do.

It is love at
first sight.

Yippity, Zippity

it's a beautiful
day.

Grandma Smiley sits on her comfortable, white wooden rocking chair watching her tired grandchildren lying on the soft rug playing with the two puppies.

She is delighted to see that her magic can bring so much happiness to her grandchildren.

What a wonderful day it has been.
Full of love, new friends, and *magic.*

♡

While waiting for their parents to arrive, Anna, Peter, Samantha, and Ryan go outside and play with Cinnamon and Blueberry Muffin on the soft, green grass.

"Here Cinnamon, catch the red ball," calls Peter. Cinnamon runs after the ball.

Ryan thinks they all look so funny he can't stop laughing.

Blueberry Muffin goes over to Samantha and licks her on the nose.

All the children are relaxed and having fun with their new friends.

♡

"Oh, what fun we had today," sighs Grandma Smiley.

"What are we going to do next week Grandma?"
asks Anna.
"It will be a special surprise for all of you," says
Grandma Smiley.

The grandchildren laugh and hug Grandma. They
run to give Cinnamon and Blueberry Muffin warm
hugs before they leave. The puppies snuggle into
their arms and wag their tails.

Grandma Smiley's Recipe for

Blueberry Muffin

2 tsp.	Memories of 2 beloved puppies
4 tsp.	Love for her grandchildren
1 cup	Sweet, plump blueberries
1 pinch	Stars for the sparkle
2 cups	Red Hearts for the love of children
1 pinch	Grandma Smiley's *Magic*

This is book two in the series of the
'My Magic Muffin' family.
Book one – Grandma Smiley's Gift of Magic
Book two – Grandma Smiley's Magical Friends

Who do you think the next
My Magic Muffin®
will be?

Blueberry Muffin

www.ingramcontent.com/pod-product-compliance
Lightning Source LLC
Chambersburg PA
CBHW050633150426
42811CB00052B/785